WE

BY **ALICE SCHERTLE**

ILLUSTRATED BY **KENNETH ADDISON**

LEE & LOW BOOKS INC. NEW YORK

AUTHOR'S NOTE

This book was inspired by discoveries of the oldest fossilized remains of humans and pre-humans ever found, discoveries made in Africa. Scientists studying these fossils have begun to piece together the story of human origins and eventual migration from Africa to all parts of the globe. It is a story that will never be fully told, since much of the evidence of our most ancient ancestors is lost to us forever. Still, thousands of fossils lie buried in the earth, waiting to be found. Where will they fit into the puzzle? What will they add to the story of our fascinating, unruly, gloriously diverse, and complex human family?

WEB SITES OF INTEREST

becominghuman.org
mnh.si.edu/anthro/humanorigins
nationalgeographic.com/outpost
ucmp.berkeley.edu

AUTHOR'S SOURCES

Berger, Lee R. *In the Footsteps of Eve: The Mystery of Human Origins.* Washington, D.C.: National Geographic, 2000.
Diamond, Jared. *Guns, Germs, and Steel: The Fates of Human Societies.* New York: W.W. Norton, 1999.
———. *The Third Chimpanzee: The Evolution and Future of the Human Animal.* New York: HarperCollins, 1992.
McKie, Robin. *Dawn of Man: The Story of Human Evolution.* New York: Dorling Kindersley, 2000.
Tattersall, Ian. *Becoming Human: Evolution and Human Uniqueness.* New York: Harcourt Brace, 1998.
Wells, Spencer. *The Journey of Man: A Genetic Odyssey.* New York: Random House, 2003.

Text copyright © 2007 by Alice Schertle
Illustrations copyright © 2005 by Kenneth Addison
LEE & LOW BOOKS Inc., 95 Madison Avenue, New York, NY 10016
leeandlow.com
Manufactured in China
Book design by Christy Hale
Book production by The Kids at Our House
The text is set in Antique Olive
The illustrations are rendered in mixed-media collage
Photographs incorporated into page 29 illustration from Dreamstime.com
10 9 8 7 6 5 4 3 2 1
First Edition

Library of Congress Cataloging-in-Publication Data
Schertle, Alice.
We / by Alice Schertle ; illustrated by Kenneth Addison.— 1st ed.
p. cm.
Summary: "Describes the emergence of humankind out of Africa, charting the course of
human development from seven million years ago to today, highlighting the development
of diversity among peoples and our ability to invent and discover"—Provided by publisher.
ISBN-13: 978-1-58430-060-1
1. Human evolution—Juvenile literature. I. Addison, Kenneth (Kenneth L.), ill. II. Title.
GN281.S277 2007
599.93'8—dc22   2005015554

To the whole family—A.S.

To my rocks, Nora Lee, Paloma, Win, Diane, and My Strong Tower—K.A.

Slowly,
layer by layer
the river carved its shallow bed
deep into the soil of Africa
undercurrents moved the brown mud downstream
water wore away stone
slowly   the river broadened its bed
into a valley

African sun warmed us
African winds blew through our thick hair
We cooled our feet and our throats in the river
and ate what we could catch   or find
in Africa

And we changed   slowly
as the river-washed stones grew smooth as moons

We were brainier now
and our hands   fingers and thumbs   so clever

A few of us stood up straight   and looked around
There was a lot to see this way
and our clever hands were free
to change things

We walked   upright
out of the valley   across the savanna
up over mountains
over plains and prairies   across deserts
through forests

until we came to the sea
and that stopped us

So we built boats
and made sails to catch the wind
and were lost on the vastness of the sea

until we found another place   and another

Here and there we stopped to build a house
and plant a seed and make a fish hook and a water jug
and to die   and be born

We harnessed the speed of horses
the patience of oxen
the endurance of camels
the strength of elephants

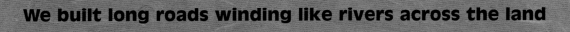

We built long roads winding like rivers across the land

When we came to a place where the sun was weak
and a river was a road of ice
we made jackets and boots and greatcoats
and hats that covered our ears
We shut the doors of our houses
and sealed the cracks against the wind

We built cities with strong walls
and machines to knock down the strong walls of cities

We made war

We made prayers and built holy places
to hold our prayers

We made music

We drew pictures and carved statues

We wrote poems and plays and books   many books

We made elevators and park benches and four-poster beds and
donuts and bicycle pumps and umbrellas and
baseball bats and saxophones and backpacks and
mouse pads and hang gliders

And then
when the seas were busy with our ships
and the skies were loud with our planes
when our homes dotted the deserts and the prairies
and the mountains
and the forests

we wondered what was at the bottom
of the deepest ocean
so we went there
to see

And we peered into our own bodies
to see what it was
we were made of

we looked through instruments
and wondered about other worlds

And some of us
returned to the water-carved canyon
to find our bones

But we had forgotten
the river running slow and cool
and the African wind in our hair
in the first place